FLATBREADS, WRAPS & MORE

RECIPES FOR APPETIZERS, PIZZAS & SNACKS

Publications International, Ltd.

Microwave Cooking: Microwave ovens vary in wattage. Use the cooking times as guidelines and check for doneness before adding more time.

Preparation/Cooking Times: Preparation times are based on the approximate amount of time required to assemble the recipe before cooking, baking, chilling or serving. These times include preparation steps such as measuring, chopping and mixing. The fact that some preparations and cooking can be done simultaneously is taken into account. Preparation of optional ingredients and serving suggestions is not included.

TABLE OF CONTENTS

pil

Publications International, Ltd.

HAWAIIAN BREAKFAST WRAP

6 **eggs**

¼ **cup milk or water**

¼ **cup chopped ham or Canadian bacon**

¼ **cup chopped red or green bell pepper**

2 **tablespoons butter or margarine**

1 **can (8 oz.) DOLE® Crushed Pineapple, drained**

4 **(8-inch) flour tortillas**

1. Beat together eggs and milk in medium bowl until blended. Set aside.

2. Cook ham and bell pepper in hot butter over medium heat in large nonstick skillet until ham is lightly browned and pepper is tender-crisp. Stir in egg mixture and crushed pineapple. Scramble until desired doneness, stirring constantly.

3. Evenly divide egg mixture onto flour tortillas. Roll sides up. Serve with watermelon wedges and lime slice, if desired.

Makes 4 servings

Variation: Place mixture on toasted English muffins to serve as a sandwich.

Prep Time: 15 min.

BREAKFAST FLATS

8 slices bacon, diced

1 package (14 ounces) refrigerated pizza dough

All-purpose flour, for dusting

1½ cups (6 ounces) shredded medium Cheddar cheese

4 eggs, fried

Kosher salt and black pepper (optional)

1. Preheat oven to 400°F. Line two baking sheets with parchment paper.

2. Warm large nonstick skillet over medium-high heat. Add bacon; cook until crisp and mostly rendered, about 8 minutes, stirring occasionally. Transfer to paper towel-lined plate to drain.

3. Divide pizza dough into 4 equal portions. Roll out on lightly floured surface into rectangles roughly 8½×4 inches. Place rolled dough onto prepared baking sheets; topping each evenly with cheese and bacon. Bake 10 minutes or until crust is golden brown and crisp and cheese is melted.

4. Spray large skillet with nonstick cooking spray. Fry eggs, sunny-side up. Keep warm.

5. Top baked flats with fried egg; season with salt and pepper, if desired. Serve immediately.

Makes 4 servings

SMOKED SALMON LAVASH

4 ounces cream cheese, softened

1 tablespoon lemon juice

¼ teaspoon prepared horseradish

4 small (about 5 inches) lavash* flatbreads

4 ounces sliced smoked salmon

½ red onion, thinly sliced

2 tablespoons capers, drained

*Lavash (also spelled "lahvosh") is a thin, crisp, Middle Eastern flat bread. Other flatbreads or toasts may be substituted.

Combine cream cheese, lemon juice and horseradish in small bowl. Spread carefully over lavash. Top with salmon, onion and capers.

Makes 4 servings

BREAKFAST PEPPERONI FLATS

2 flatbreads

1 cup (4 ounces) shredded mozzarella cheese

2 plum tomatoes, diced

24 slices turkey pepperoni, cut into quarters

2 teaspoons grated Parmesan cheese

¼ to ½ cup chopped fresh basil

1. Preheat oven to 425°F. Place flatbreads on large baking sheet. Sprinkle evenly with mozzarella cheese, tomatoes, turkey pepperoni and Parmesan cheese.

2. Bake 3 minutes or until cheese is melted. Remove from oven. Sprinkle with basil. Let stand on baking sheet 2 minutes before cutting.

Makes 4 servings

EGG AND BACON BRUNCH WRAPS

1 cup cholesterol-free egg
   substitute

¼ cup shredded Parmesan
   cheese

2 slices Canadian bacon,
   diced

½ teaspoon hot pepper
   sauce

¼ teaspoon black pepper

4 (7-inch) red chile tortillas
   or whole wheat tortillas

1 cup baby spinach leaves

1. Preheat oven to 325°F. Combine egg substitute, cheese, bacon, hot pepper sauce and black pepper in bowl. Pour into 9-inch glass baking dish sprayed with butter-flavored cooking spray. Bake 15 minutes or until egg substitute is set. Remove from oven.

2. Place tortillas in oven 1 minute or until soft and pliable. Cut egg substitute into quarters. Place 1 wedge in center of each tortilla. Top with ¼ cup spinach leaves. Fold bottom of tortilla to center; fold sides to center to enclose filling and serve immediately.

Makes 4 servings

Note: Canadian bacon comes from the loin of the pig. It is much more meaty and has less fat than traditional bacon. As a result, it tastes more like ham in flavor.

BAKED FRENCH TOAST WITH BLUEBERRY COMPOTE

2 eggs

1 cup half-and-half

⅓ cup sugar

⅛ teaspoon salt

¾ teaspoon ground cinnamon

1½ teaspoons vanilla

6 rounds pocketless pita-type flatbread, quartered

2 cups fresh blueberries

Zest of 1 lemon, finely grated

¼ cup maple syrup

1 tablespoon fresh lemon juice

1. Whisk eggs, half-and-half, sugar, salt, cinnamon and vanilla in medium bowl until combined.

2. Arrange flatbread pieces in even layer in 9-inch pie plate. Pour egg mixture over top; cover and refrigerate overnight.

3. Preheat oven to 400°F. Bake French toast about 30 minutes or until egg mixture is set and top of flatbread is browned.

4. Meanwhile, combine blueberries, lemon zest and syrup in small saucepan over medium-high heat. Cook about 12 minutes, stirring occasionally, or until blueberries have burst and mixture has reduced to syrupy consistency. Stir in lemon juice.

5. Top French toast with blueberry compote to serve.

Makes 4 to 6 servings

CHORIZO-POTATO HASH WITH CRISP CRUMB TOPPING

1 naan bread, torn into uneven pieces

6 tablespoons plus 1 teaspoon olive oil, divided

Kosher salt and black pepper

1 pound Mexican chorizo, casings removed

1 onion, diced

1 yellow bell pepper, diced

1 red bell pepper, diced

2 Russet potatoes, peeled, shredded, rinsed and squeezed dry *or* 1 bag (1 pound 4 ounces) refrigerated shredded hash brown potatoes

1 green onion, sliced on the bias

═══ TIP ═══

This recipe is especially good to make when you have day-old or stale flatbread.

1. Place naan pieces in food processor; pulse until small crumbs form, about 15 pulses. Transfer to large bowl; toss with 2 tablespoons oil.

2. Heat large skillet over medium heat. Add crumbs; cook 6 to 8 minutes or until browned and toasted, stirring occasionally. Season with salt and black pepper; set aside.

3. Heat 1 teaspoon oil in same skillet over medium-high heat. Add chorizo; cook about 5 minutes or until browned, using spatula to break up the meat. Transfer to paper towel-lined plate. Heat 1 tablespoon oil in same skillet; add onion and bell peppers; cook about 8 minutes or until tender, stirring occasionally. Season with salt and black pepper. Transfer to bowl.

4 Heat remaining 3 tablespoons oil in same skillet; add potatoes in even layer; cook about 3 minutes or until browned and beginning to crisp on bottom. Turn potatoes, continue to cook about 10 minutes or until tender and evenly browned, stirring occasionally. Season with salt and black pepper. Stir in chorizo and onion-bell pepper mixture; cook 2 minutes until heated through. Top with pita crumbs and green onion to serve.

Makes 6 servings

SPINACH, MUSHROOM, EGG AND GRUYÈRE ROLLUPS

1 tablespoon plus
   4 teaspoons olive oil,
   divided

1 shallot, thinly sliced
   (about ½ cup)

1 bag (6 ounces) fresh baby
   spinach

1 clove garlic, minced

½ teaspoon plus ⅛ teaspoon
   salt, divided

8 ounces cremini
   mushrooms, thinly sliced

¼ teaspoon black pepper,
   divided

2 pieces flatbread,
   9½×11 inches, lightly
   toasted

⅔ cup shredded Gruyère
   cheese

6 eggs

2 tablespoons milk

2 teaspoons Dijon mustard

═══ TIP ═══
Serve at room temperature or
heat in microwave 5 to
10 seconds to warm.

1. Heat 2 teaspoons oil in large nonstick skillet over medium heat. Add shallot; cook 5 to 6 minutes until softened. Increase heat to medium-high, add spinach; cook 2 minutes until wilted. Add garlic and ¼ teaspoon salt; cook 1 minute, stirring frequently. Set aside.

2. Heat 1 tablespoon oil in same skillet over medium-high heat. Add mushrooms, ¼ teaspoon salt and ⅛ teaspoon pepper; cook 6 minutes until browned, stirring occasionally.

3. Place half of spinach-mushroom mixture on each flatbread; top with cheese.

4. Whisk eggs in large bowl. Add remaining ⅛ teaspoon salt, ⅛ teaspoon pepper, milk and mustard.

5. Heat remaining 2 teaspoons oil in same skillet over medium-high heat. Add egg mixture; cook about 1 minute, stirring frequently, or until eggs are set but not dry.

6. Place cooked eggs on spinach; roll up flatbread. Cut on bias to serve.

Makes 4 servings

PERFECT FOR A PARTY

CHICKEN, HUMMUS AND VEGETABLE WRAPS

¾ cup hummus (regular, roasted red pepper or roasted garlic)

4 (8- to 10-inch) sun-dried tomato or spinach wraps *or* whole wheat tortillas

2 cups chopped cooked chicken breast

Chipotle hot pepper sauce or Louisiana-style hot pepper sauce (optional)

½ cup shredded carrots

½ cup chopped unpeeled cucumber

½ cup thinly sliced radishes

2 tablespoons chopped fresh mint *or* basil

Spread hummus evenly over wraps all the way to edges. Arrange chicken over hummus; sprinkle with hot pepper sauce, if desired. Top with carrots, cucumber, radishes and mint. Roll up tightly. Cut in half diagonally.

Makes 4 servings

Variation: Substitute alfalfa sprouts for the radishes. For tasty appetizers, cut wraps into bite-size pieces.

WILD MUSHROOM FLATBREAD

1 package (about 14 ounces) refrigerated pizza dough

2 teaspoons olive oil

1 package (4 ounces) sliced cremini mushrooms

1 package (4 ounces) sliced shiitake mushrooms

1 shallot, thinly sliced

2 cloves garlic, minced

½ teaspoon salt

¾ cup (3 ounces) grated Gruyère cheese

2 teaspoons chopped fresh thyme

1. Preheat oven to 400°F. Line baking sheet with parchment paper. Spray with nonstick cooking spray.

2. Roll out pizza dough on lightly floured surface to 15×10-inch rectangle. Place on prepared baking sheet. Bake 10 minutes.

3. Meanwhile, heat oil in large nonstick skillet over medium-high heat. Add mushrooms; cook and stir 5 minutes. Add shallot and garlic; cook and stir 5 minutes or until tender. Season with salt.

4. Arrange mushroom mixture evenly over prepared pizza crust. Top evenly with cheese and thyme.

5. Bake 8 minutes or until cheese is melted. To serve, cut into 16 pieces.

Makes 8 servings

WHOLE WHEAT FLATBREAD WITH HERBED RICOTTA, PEACHES AND ARUGULA

½ cup ricotta cheese

½ teaspoon coarse salt

⅛ teaspoon black pepper

2 tablespoons finely chopped fresh basil

2 whole wheat naan breads

1 ripe peach, cut into 12 slices

½ cup arugula

½ teaspoon lemon juice

1 teaspoon extra virgin olive oil

2 teaspoons balsamic vinegar

Flaky sea salt, for sprinkling

1. Preheat oven to 400°F. Line baking sheet with parchment paper.

2. Combine ricotta cheese, coarse salt, pepper and basil in small bowl. Spread mixture evenly on each piece of naan. Arrange peaches on top. Bake 12 minutes or until bottom of naan is crisp.

3. Combine arugula, lemon juice and oil in medium bowl; toss gently. Top baked flatbreads with arugula. Drizzle with vinegar and sprinkle with sea salt.

4. Cut each flatbread into quarters to serve.

Makes 4 servings

ONION AND SHRIMP FLATBREAD PIZZA WITH GOAT CHEESE

4 teaspoons olive oil, divided

3 large onions, thinly sliced

¼ teaspoon salt

1 package (about 14 ounces) refrigerated pizza crust dough

½ pound raw small shrimp, peeled

⅛ cup chopped fresh chives

3 ounces goat cheese, crumbled

½ teaspoon black pepper (optional)

1. Heat 2 teaspoons oil in large skillet over medium heat. Add onions; cook and stir about 8 minutes. Stir in salt. Reduce heat to medium-low; cook, stirring occasionally, 25 minutes or until onions are soft and caramelized. If onions are cooking too fast, reduce heat to low.

2. Meanwhile, preheat oven to 425°F. Roll out dough on 15×10-inch baking sheet. Bake 8 to 10 minutes or until golden brown. Turn off oven. Spread caramelized onions over crust.

3. Heat remaining 2 teaspoons oil in same skillet over medium heat. Cook and stir shrimp 2 minutes or until pink and opaque. Arrange shrimp over onions on pizza. Sprinkle with chives, goat cheese and pepper, if desired.

4. Place pizza in warm oven 1 to 2 minutes or until cheese is soft. Cut into 12 squares.

Makes 6 servings

SUN-DRIED TOMATO, CHICKEN SAUSAGE, FENNEL AND APPLE FLATBREAD

1 (10½-ounce) stone-baked pizza crust*

2 tablespoons sun-dried tomato dressing

1 small red onion, thinly sliced

½ fennel bulb, thinly sliced

1 fully-cooked sun-dried tomato chicken sausage, thinly sliced

1 Granny Smith apple, peeled, cored and thinly sliced

¾ cup finely shredded mozzarella cheese

2 tablespoons grated Parmesan cheese

If unavailable, may substitute with a 12-inch prepared pizza crust.

1. Heat oven to 400°F. Spread dressing over crust.

2. Layer onion, fennel, chicken sausage and apple over crust.

3. Sprinkle evenly with cheeses. Bake 20 minutes or until cheeses melt and crust edges are brown.

Makes 6 servings

WHOLE WHEAT FLATBREADS WITH TOMATO-AVOCADO SALSA

SALSA

- 1½ **cups plum tomatoes, seeded and finely chopped**
- 1 **avocado, cut into ¼-inch cubes**
- ¼ **cup red onion, finely chopped**
- 1 to 2 **tablespoons finely chopped jalapeño pepper***
- 1 **tablespoon lemon juice**
- 2 **tablespoons fresh cilantro, finely chopped**
- ¼ **teaspoon salt**

FLATBREADS

- 2 **cups white whole wheat flour** *or* 1¾ **cups whole wheat flour and** ¼ **cup white flour**
- ¼ **teaspoon salt**
- ⅞ **to 1 cup water**
- ½ **cup all-purpose flour for rolling**
- 2 **tablespoons melted butter (optional)**

*Jalapeño peppers can sting and irritate the skin, so wear rubber gloves when handling peppers and do not touch your eyes.

1. Combine salsa ingredients in medium bowl. Cover and let chill.

2. To make flatbreads, mix white whole wheat flour and salt in medium bowl. Make a well in center of flour. Add water gradually while mixing dough. (Depending on the type of flour, the amount of water needed may vary slightly.) (Dough should be soft and easy to roll into a ball.) Knead dough 1 to 2 minutes until smooth and elastic. Cover and let sit 10 minutes or longer.

3. Preheat oven to broil. Lightly spray baking sheets with nonstick cooking spray. Place ½ cup all-purpose flour, for rolling, in shallow container.

4. Divide dough into 8 balls. Press to flatten. Roll each flat ball in flour. Then roll each flat ball into approximately ¼-inch-thick oval.

5. Place 3 to 4 flatbreads on baking sheet. Broil 2 to 3 minutes (the flatbreads will puff) about 5 to 6 inches from heat source until top is light brown. Turn over and broil 1 to 2 minutes until light brown. If desired, lightly brush tops of flatbreads with melted butter to keep them moist. Serve immediately or place in airtight container to serve later. Just before serving, top with salsa.

Makes 8 servings

LAVASH CHIPS WITH ARTICHOKE PESTO

3 pieces lavash bread, each 7½×9½ inches

¼ cup plus 2 tablespoons olive oil, divided

¾ teaspoon kosher salt, divided

1 can (14 ounces) artichoke hearts, rinsed and drained

½ cup chopped walnuts, toasted*

¼ cup packed fresh basil leaves

1 clove garlic, minced

2 tablespoons lemon juice

¼ cup grated Parmesan cheese

To toast walnuts, spread in single layer on baking sheet. Toast in preheated 350°F oven 6 to 8 minutes or until golden brown, stirring frequently.

1. Preheat oven to 350°F. Line 2 baking sheets with parchment paper. Set two oven racks to upper third and lower third of oven.

2. Brush both sides of each piece lavash with 2 tablespoons oil. Sprinkle with ¼ teaspoon salt. Bake 10 minutes, rotating and alternating baking sheets between upper and lower racks, until lavash is crisp and browned. Remove from oven; set on wire rack to cool completely.

3. Place artichoke hearts, walnuts, basil, garlic, lemon juice and ½ teaspoon salt in food processor; pulse about 12 times until coarsely chopped. While food processor is running, slowly stream remaining ¼ cup oil until emulsified. Add cheese and pulse until blended.

4. Break lavash into chips. Serve with pesto.

Makes 6 servings (about 1½ cups pesto)

SMOKED SALMON SPIRALS

2 tablespoons cream cheese

1 light sun-dried tomato flatbread

2 ounces smoked salmon (lox)

½ cup baby arugula

½ cup thinly sliced red bell pepper

Spread cream cheese on flatbread. Layer with smoked salmon, arugula and bell pepper. Roll up jelly-roll style. To serve, cut into 6 pieces.

Makes 2 servings

RAMEN SHRIMP & ALFREDO FLATBREAD

FLATBREAD

4 packages (3 ounces each) shrimp-flavored ramen noodles

4 eggs

½ teaspoon garlic powder

TOPPING

1 container (15 ounces) prepared alfredo sauce

1 container (about 8 ounces) sun-dried tomato pesto

12 ounces small cooked shrimp

1 cup shredded 4-cheese Italian blend

¼ cup grated Parmesan cheese

¼ cup chopped fresh parsley

1. Preheat oven to 400°F. Line large 15×10-inch baking sheet or jelly-roll pan with foil. Spray with nonstick cooking spray.

2. Break each package of noodles into 4 pieces. Cook according to package directions using seasoning packets. Drain well.

3. Combine noodles, eggs and garlic powder in large bowl. Place noodle mixture on prepared baking sheet; press into thin layer, about ½-inch thick. Bake 13 to 18 minutes or until set. Remove from oven; let stand 30 minutes to cool completely and firm up.

4. Preheat broiler. Combine alfredo sauce and pesto in large bowl; spoon evenly over cooled noodles. Top with shrimp and cheeses. Place on middle rack; broil 6 minutes or until cheese is lightly golden. Remove from oven; sprinkle with parsley. Let stand 10 minutes before cutting.

Makes 24 pieces

GOAT CHEESE, CARAMELIZED ONIONS AND PROSCIUTTO FLATBREAD BITES

2 tablespoons olive oil, plus additional for drizzle

1 onion, sliced

¼ teaspoon salt

¼ cup water

All-purpose flour, for dusting

1 package (about 14 ounces) refrigerated pizza dough

2 ounces goat cheese

4 slices prosciutto

½ teaspoon fresh thyme leaves

1. Preheat oven to 450°F. Line baking sheet with parchment paper.

2. Heat 2 tablespoons oil in large skillet over medium heat. Add onion and salt; cook about 18 to 20 minutes or until onion caramelizes, stirring occasionally and adding water halfway through cooking.

3. Roll pizza dough on lightly floured surface into two 9×5-inch rectangles; transfer dough to prepared baking sheet. Top each with onions, goat cheese and prosciutto.

4. Bake 12 minutes or until crust is golden brown and prosciutto is crisp.

5. Drizzle with additional oil and sprinkle with thyme. Cut each into 12 portions.

Makes 6 servings

LUNCH & DINNER IDEAS

ASIAN CILANTRO WRAPS

SAUCE

- 2 tablespoons raspberry or strawberry fruit spread
- 2 tablespoons soy sauce
- ⅛ teaspoon red pepper flakes

FILLING

- 2 teaspoons canola oil
- 3 cups thinly sliced purple cabbage
- 6 ounces asparagus spears, trimmed and cut into ½-inch pieces (about 1½ cups)
- ½ cup thinly sliced carrots
- 1 cup chopped green onions, green and white parts (about 8 green onions)
- 4 (6-inch) flour tortillas, warmed
- ¼ cup chopped fresh cilantro
- ¼ cup chopped peanuts
- 1 cup diced cooked chicken breast

1. Microwave fruit spread in small microwavable bowl on HIGH 15 seconds or until slightly melted. Stir in soy sauce and red pepper flakes; set aside.

2. Heat oil in large nonstick skillet over medium-high heat. Add cabbage, asparagus and carrots; cook and stir 2 minutes. Add green onions; cook and stir 2 to 3 minutes or until cabbage is slightly wilted. Remove from heat.

3. Spoon about 1 cup filling on each tortilla. Top each with 1 tablespoon sauce, 1 tablespoon cilantro, 1 tablespoon peanuts and ¼ cup chicken. Roll up to enclose filling.

Makes 4 servings

STUFFED FOCACCIA SANDWICH

1 container (about
  5 ounces) soft cheese
  with garlic and herbs

1 (10-inch) round herb or
  onion focaccia, cut in
  half horizontally

½ cup thinly sliced red onion

½ cup coarsely chopped
  pimiento-stuffed green
  olives, drained

¼ cup sliced mild banana
  pepper

4 ounces thinly sliced deli
  hard salami

6 ounces thinly sliced oven-
  roasted turkey breast

1 package (⅔ ounce) fresh
  basil, stems removed

1. Spread soft cheese over cut sides of focaccia. Layer bottom half evenly with remaining ingredients. Cover sandwich with top half of focaccia; press down firmly.

2. Cut sandwich into 4 equal pieces. Serve immediately or wrap individually in plastic wrap and refrigerate until serving time.

Makes 4 sandwiches

TIP

This sandwich is great for make-ahead lunches or picnics.

SPICY SMOKED TURKEY CLUB FLATOUT® WRAP

- 1 Flatout® Light Flatbread
- 1 ounce fat-free creamy ranch dressing
- 1 tablespoon hot salsa
- 1 leaf romaine lettuce
- 2 tomato slices (optional)
- 7 pepper rings (optional)
- 3 ounces BUTTERBALL® Honey Roasted and Smoked Turkey Breast, thinly sliced
- 2 slices BUTTERBALL® Turkey Bacon, cooked
- 1 slice reduced-fat pepper jack cheese

Combine dressing and salsa; spread over entire Flatout. On one rounded end, layer romaine,and, if desired, tomatoes and pepper rings. Add turkey, turkey bacon and cheese. Starting with layered end, roll up tightly. Cut before serving.

Makes 1 serving

Prep Time: 5 minutes
Total Time: 10 minutes

MUFFULETTA

1 (12-ounce) loaf focaccia
    bread
3 tablespoons prepared
    Italian salad dressing
½ cup sliced Spanish olives
8 ounces thinly sliced salami
    or baked ham
4 ounces thinly sliced
    provolone or sharp
    Cheddar cheese
    Lettuce leaves

1. Cut bread crosswise into halves; brush cut sides of both halves generously with salad dressing. Pour any remaining salad dressing over olives.

2. Arrange meat and cheese on bottom half of bread; top with olives, lettuce leaves and top half of bread. Cut into wedges to serve.

Makes 4 servings

Lighten Up: To reduce the amount of fat in this recipe, replace the Italian salad dressing with reduced-fat or fat-free Italian salad dressing.

41

PACIFIC RIM WRAPS WITH CREAMY CITRUS GINGER DRESSING

DRESSING

- ⅔ cup (5 fluid-ounce can) **NESTLÉ® CARNATION® Evaporated Milk**
- 5 tablespoons lemon juice
- ¼ cup vegetable oil
- 3 tablespoons granulated sugar
- 2 teaspoons ground ginger
- 1 teaspoon salt
- ¼ teaspoon ground black pepper

SALAD

- 1 package (6.5 ounces) or 4 cups washed salad greens
- 3 cups shredded, cooked chicken (about 2 to 3 boneless chicken breast halves)
- 1 cup matchstick or shredded carrots
- 1 cup fresh sugar snap pea pods, cut in half
- ½ cup sweetened dried cranberries
- ¼ cup toasted slivered almonds (optional)
- 6 (8-inch) flour tortillas

FOR DRESSING

PLACE evaporated milk, lemon juice, oil, sugar, ginger, salt and black pepper in small jar or resealable container; cover with lid. Shake well until blended. Makes 1 cup.

FOR SALAD

COMBINE salad greens, chicken, carrots, sugar snap peas, dried cranberries and almonds in large bowl. Add ⅔ *cup* dressing; toss until evenly coated.

PLACE *1 cup* salad mixture on each tortilla. Roll up tightly. Cut in half and serve along with *remaining* dressing, if desired. Or, wrap each in wax paper, foil or plastic wrap and refrigerate to eat later.

Makes 6 servings

Prep Time: 10 minutes

TIPS

- Dressing can be made a day ahead and refrigerated. Shake well before using.
- Use pre-cooked grilled chicken strips to save time.
- Look for pre-packaged matchstick carrots in your local store's produce section.

MEXICALI TURKEY WRAPS

1 container (about 6 ounces) prepared guacamole

6 (8-inch) whole wheat flour tortillas

1½ cups shredded lettuce

1½ cups shredded leftover cooked BUTTERBALL® Turkey

6 tablespoons canned black beans, rinsed and drained

6 tablespoons frozen corn, thawed and drained

6 tablespoons prepared salsa

6 tablespoons crumbled queso fresco cheese

1. Spread 2 tablespoons guacamole evenly over each tortilla to within ¼ inch of edge.

2. Sprinkle each tortilla evenly with ¼ cup lettuce; press lettuce into guacamole lightly. Top each with ¼ cup turkey and 1 tablespoon each beans, corn, salsa and cheese.

3. Roll up tortillas tightly. Cut diagonally in half.

Makes 6 servings

Prep Time: 20 minutes

CALIFORNIA CHICKEN WRAP

3 tablespoons HELLMANN'S® or BEST FOODS® Mayonnaise Dressing with Olive Oil

4 (6-inch) fajita size whole wheat flour tortillas

12 ounces boneless, skinless chicken breasts, grilled and sliced

1 medium avocado, peeled and sliced

1 red bell pepper, sliced

½ cup sliced red onion

2 cups mixed salad greens

1. **Spread It:** Spread HELLMANN'S® or BEST FOODS® Mayonnaise Dressing with Olive Oil.

2. **Stuff It:** Layer chicken, avocado, red pepper, red onion and salad greens down center of each tortilla.

3. **Wrap It:** Roll and fold the filled tortilla.

Makes 4 servings

Note: Also terrific with HELLMANN'S® or BEST FOODS® Real Mayonnaise or HELLMANN'S® or BEST FOODS® Light Mayonnaise.

Prep Time: 10 minutes

45

BEEF AND VEGGIE FLATBREAD

½ **pound lean ground beef**

1 **medium clove garlic, minced**

1 **loaf (11 ounces) refrigerated French bread dough**

½ **cup tomato sauce**

1 **teaspoon dried oregano**

¼ **teaspoon red pepper flakes (optional)**

12 **slices (about ¾ ounce) turkey pepperoni, halved**

2 **ounces sliced mushrooms**

¼ **cup chopped fresh basil**

½ **cup thinly sliced green bell pepper**

½ **cup thinly sliced yellow onion**

½ **cup (2 ounces) shredded mozzarella cheese**

2 **teaspoons grated Parmesan cheese**

1. Preheat oven to 425°F.

2. Heat medium nonstick skillet over medium-high heat until hot, then coat skillet with nonstick cooking spray. Add beef and garlic; cook until no longer pink, stirring constantly. Drain excess fat; set aside.

3. Coat large baking sheet with cooking spray. Unroll bread dough onto clean work surface; cut into four equal pieces. Roll out and place on prepared baking sheet.

4. Spoon 2 tablespoons tomato sauce onto each flatbread; sprinkle with oregano and red pepper flakes. Equally divide pepperoni and beef among flatbreads. Top with mushrooms, basil, bell pepper, onion and mozzarella cheese. Bake 10 minutes or until golden brown on the edges. Sprinkle with Parmesan cheese.

Makes 4 servings

SHRIMP AND SPINACH PITA PIZZA

½ **teaspoon olive oil**

¼ **cup thinly sliced red onion**

3 **cups chopped fresh spinach**

¼ **teaspoon dried oregano**

1 **cup (4 ounces) SARGENTO® Shredded Reduced Fat Mozzarella Cheese, divided**

2 **(6-inch) pita breads**

2 **plum tomatoes, sliced**

10 **large shrimp, cooked and peeled**

- Heat oil in small skillet over medium heat. Cook onion 1 minute. Add spinach and oregano; cook 1 minute or until spinach is wilted. Sprinkle ¼ cup cheese on each piece of pita bread. Top with spinach mixture, tomatoes, shrimp and remaining cheese.

- Place pitas on baking sheet; bake in preheated 400°F oven 10 minutes or until cheese is melted.

Makes 2 servings

Prep Time: 10 minutes
Cook Time: 10 minutes

INDIVIDUAL MEXICAN PIZZAS

4 (7- to 8-inch) flour tortillas

2 teaspoons canola or
   vegetable oil

1 teaspoon chili powder

2 cups shredded or chopped
   cooked chicken

1 cup rinsed and drained
   canned black beans

1 cup diced well-drained
   bottled roasted red
   peppers

½ cup sliced green onions

1¾ cups (7 ounces)
   SARGENTO® Traditional
   Cut Shredded Pepper
   Jack Cheese

   Sour cream or guacamole
   (optional)

- Place tortillas on a foil-lined baking sheet. Brush oil and sprinkle chili powder over tortillas. Bake in preheated 375°F oven 9 to 10 minutes or until crisp and golden brown. (If tortillas puff up during baking, press down with a wide spatula).

- Top tortillas with chicken, beans, red peppers, green onions and cheese.

- Return to oven; bake 10 to 12 minutes or until heated through and cheese is melted. Cut each tortilla into 4 to 6 wedges. Serve with sour cream or guacamole, if desired.

Makes 4 servings

Prep Time: 15 minutes
Cook Time: 22 minutes

GRILLED BUFFALO CHICKEN WRAPS

4 boneless skinless chicken
  breasts (about 4 ounces
  each)

¼ cup plus 2 tablespoons
  buffalo wing sauce,
  divided

2 cups broccoli slaw mix

1 tablespoon blue cheese
  salad dressing

4 (8-inch) whole wheat
  tortillas, warmed

1. Place chicken in large resealable food storage bag. Add ¼ cup buffalo sauce; seal bag. Marinate in refrigerator 15 minutes.

2. Meanwhile, prepare grill for direct cooking over medium-high heat. Grill chicken 5 to 6 minutes per side or until no longer pink. When cool enough to handle, slice chicken and combine with remaining 2 tablespoons buffalo sauce in medium bowl.

3. Combine slaw and dressing in medium bowl; mix well.

4. Arrange chicken and slaw evenly down center of each tortilla. Roll up to secure filling. To serve, cut in half diagonally.

Makes 4 servings

TIP

If you don't like the spicy flavor of buffalo wing sauce, substitute your favorite barbecue sauce.

RUSTIC ROASTED RED PEPPER, ROSEMARY AND PANCETTA FLATBREAD

1 can (11 ounces) refrigerated thin pizza crust

2 tablespoons sun-dried tomato dressing

1 large yellow onion, thinly sliced

2 ounces pancetta,* chopped

2 cloves garlic, crushed

1 jar (7 ounces) roasted red peppers in water, drained and sliced

1 tablespoon chopped fresh rosemary

¼ cup shredded Parmesan cheese

Pancetta is Italian bacon. Unlike American bacon, which is most often smoked, pancetta is unsmoked pork belly that's cured in salt and spices such as nutmeg, black pepper and fennel. It's then dried for a few months. If you can't find pancetta, you may use 2 ounces of bacon instead.

1. Heat oven to 400°F. Unroll pizza crust on baking sheet sprayed with nonstick cooking spray. Fold edges over to form ½-inch rim. Bake 5 minutes.

2. Place dressing in large nonstick skillet heated over medium heat. Add onion and cook 6 minutes. Add pancetta and garlic; cook an additional 4 minutes. Spread over pizza crust.

3. Layer peppers on pizza. Sprinkle with rosemary and cheese. Bake 10 minutes or until cheese melts and crust edges are brown.

Makes 6 servings

Note: Buy roasted red peppers in water and not oil—check ingredients to be sure.

Tip: Kitchen scissors are a great tool for cutting pizzas and flatbreads—neater and easier to handle than a pizza cutter.

GRILLED STEAK AND FRESH MOZZARELLA FLATBREAD

1 to 1¼ pounds beef Top Sirloin Filets, cut 1 inch thick, tied

1½ teaspoons lemon pepper

2 cups packed fresh baby spinach

¼ pound fresh mozzarella cheese, cut into ½-inch pieces (¾ cup)

2 tablespoons chopped fresh basil

1½ teaspoons balsamic vinegar

4 naan breads (Indian flatbread) or pita breads

1. Press lemon pepper evenly onto steaks. Place steaks on grid over medium, ash-covered coals. Grill, covered, 12 to 17 minutes (over medium heat on preheated gas grill, 12 to 16 minutes) for medium rare (145°F) to medium (160°F) doneness, turning occasionally.

2. Meanwhile, combine spinach, cheese and basil in large bowl. Drizzle with balsamic vinegar; toss to coat and set aside.

3. Remove steak from grill and let stand 5 minutes. Place naan on grill; grill, covered, 1 to 3 minutes or until lightly browned, turning once.

4. Carve steaks into slices. Top naan evenly with spinach mixture and steak slices.

Makes 4 servings

courtesy of The Beef Checkoff

GRILLED STEAK AND BLUE CHEESE FLATBREADS

1 (4-ounce) filet mignon

¼ teaspoon garlic powder

⅛ teaspoon salt

⅛ teaspoon black pepper

2 blue cheese spreadable cheese wedges (about 1 ounce each)

2 flatbreads

½ cup thinly sliced tomato

¼ cup thinly sliced red onion

2 tablespoons crumbled blue cheese

½ cup baby arugula

Balsamic vinegar (optional)

1. Prepare grill for direct cooking over medium heat.

2. Season beef with garlic powder, salt and pepper. Grill 5 minutes per side or until medium rare or desired doneness. Remove to plate. Let stand 5 minutes. Reduce heat to low.

3. Slice beef into thin slices. Spread 1 cheese wedge onto each flatbread. Top evenly with beef, tomato and onion. Sprinkle with blue cheese.

4. Grill, covered, 8 to 10 minutes or until crisp and heated through. Top with arugula just before serving. Drizzle with balsamic vinegar, if desired.

Makes 2 servings

BBQ CHICKEN CRISPBREAD PIZZAS

1 package (3 ounces) ramen
   noodles, any flavor*

¼ cup prepared barbecue
   sauce

½ cup chopped cooked
   chicken breast

2 tablespoons chopped
   green onion

¼ cup shredded Cheddar
   cheese

Discard seasoning packet.

1. Preheat oven to 400°F. Line baking sheet with foil. Break noodles horizontally into 2 pieces. Place on prepared baking sheet. Bake noodles 4 minutes to lightly toast.

2. Spread barbecue sauce over noodles. Layer chicken and onion on sauce; sprinkle with cheese.

3. Bake 4 minutes or until cheese melts and noodles begin to brown.

Makes 2 servings

OPEN-FACED LAMB NAAN SANDWICHES WITH RAITA

1 tablespoon olive oil

1 red onion, diced

1 pound ground lamb

1¼ teaspoons minced garlic, divided

1 tablespoon tomato paste

1 teaspoon ground cumin

½ teaspoon ground corinader

1¾ teaspoons kosher salt, divided

¼ cup diced English cucumber

¾ cup (6 ounces) nonfat plain Greek yogurt

2 tablespoons chopped fresh cilantro

4 pieces naan bread, lightly toasted

1. Heat oil in large skillet over medium heat. Add onion; cook about 8 to 10 minutes or until softened. Transfer to small bowl.

2. Cook lamb in same skillet over medium-high heat about 8 minutes or until browned, stirring occasionally. Add 1 teaspoon garlic, tomato paste, cumin, coriander and 1 teaspoon salt; cook 1 minute, stirring constantly. Add onion; cook 1 minute.

3. Combine cucumber, yogurt, remaining ¼ teaspoon garlic, cilantro and remaining ¾ teaspoon salt in medium bowl.

4. Divide lamb evenly among warmed naan; top with raita. Serve immediately.

Makes 4 servings

BBQ CHICKEN FLATBREAD

3 tablespoons red wine vinegar

2 teaspoons sugar

¼ red onion, thinly sliced (about ⅓ cup)

3 cups shredded rotisserie chicken meat

½ cup barbecue sauce

1 package (about 14 ounces) refrigerated pizza dough

All-purpose flour, for dusting

1½ cups (6 ounces) shredded mozzarella cheese

1 green onion, thinly sliced on bias

2 tablespoons fresh cilantro

1. Preheat oven to 400°F; set oven rack to lower third of oven. Line baking sheet with parchment paper.

2. Combine vinegar and sugar in small bowl. Add red onion; cover and let sit at room temperature. Combine chicken and barbecue sauce in medium bowl.

3. Roll dough into 11×9-inch rectangle on lightly floured surface. Transfer dough to prepared baking sheet.

4. Top flatbread evenly with cheese and barbecue chicken mixture. Bake about 12 minutes or until crust is golden and crisp and cheese is melted. Scatter pickled red onion over top. Garnish with green onion and cilantro. Serve immediately.

Makes 4 servings

SHREDDED BEEF WRAPS

1 beef flank steak or
beef skirt steak
(1 to 1½ pounds)

1 cup beef broth

½ cup sun-dried tomatoes
(not packed in oil),
chopped

3 to 4 cloves garlic, minced

¼ teaspoon ground cumin

4 (8-inch) flour tortillas

Toppings: shredded
lettuce, diced tomatoes
and shredded Monterey
Jack cheese

SLOW COOKER DIRECTIONS

1. Cut beef into quarters. Place beef, broth, tomatoes, garlic and cumin in slow cooker. Cover; cook on LOW 7 to 8 hours or until beef shreds easily.

2. Remove beef to cutting board; shred with two forks or cut into thin strips.

3. Place remaining juices from slow cooker in blender or food processor; blend until sauce is smooth.

4. Spoon beef onto tortillas with small amount of sauce. Add desired toppings. Roll up and serve.

Makes 4 servings

DELI BEEF WRAPS WITH CREAMY HONEY-MUSTARD SPREAD

3 tablespoons mayonnaise

1 tablespoon honey mustard

1½ teaspoons packed dark brown sugar (optional)

4 whole grain or whole wheat tortillas

2 cups packed shredded lettuce

6 ounces thinly sliced deli roast beef

1 medium green bell pepper, thinly sliced

¼ cup thinly sliced red onion

1. Stir mayonnaise, honey mustard and brown sugar, if desired, in small bowl until well blended. Spread evenly on tortillas.

2. Layer lettuce, roast beef, bell pepper and onion evenly on tortillas.

3. Roll up to enclose filling. Serve immediately or refrigerate up to 6 hours.

Makes 4 wraps

Variation: Stir chopped fresh cilantro into the mayonnaise mixture and add a layer of chopped avocado.

SHREDDED PORK WRAPS

1 cup salsa, divided

2 tablespoons cornstarch

1 boneless pork loin roast
   (2 pounds)

6 (8-inch) flour tortillas

3 cups broccoli slaw mix

½ cup (2 ounces) shredded
   Cheddar cheese

SLOW COOKER DIRECTIONS

1. Combine ¼ cup salsa and cornstarch in small bowl; stir until smooth. Pour mixture into slow cooker. Top with pork roast. Pour remaining ¾ cup salsa over roast. Cover; cook on LOW 6 to 8 hours.

2. Remove pork to cutting board. Trim and discard fat. Pull pork into coarse shreds using two forks.

3. Divide shredded pork evenly among tortillas. Spoon about 2 tablespoons salsa mixture on top of pork. Top evenly with slaw and cheese. Fold bottom edge of tortilla over filling; fold in sides. Roll up completely to enclose filling. Serve remaining salsa mixture as dipping sauce.

Makes 6 servings

TORTILLA "PIZZAS"

1 can (about 14 ounces)
    Mexican-style stewed
    tomatoes, drained

1 can (10 ounces) chunk
    white chicken packed in
    water, drained

1 green onion, minced

2 teaspoons ground cumin,
    divided

½ teaspoon garlic powder

1 cup refried beans

4 tablespoons chopped
    fresh cilantro, divided

2 large flour tortillas or
    4 small flour tortillas

1 cup (4 ounces) shredded
    Monterey Jack cheese
    with jalapeño peppers

1. Preheat broiler. Combine tomatoes, chicken, green onion, 1 teaspoon cumin and garlic powder in medium bowl. Mix well; set aside.

2. Combine beans, remaining 1 teaspoon cumin and 2 tablespoons cilantro in small bowl. Set aside.

3. Place tortillas on baking sheet. Broil 30 seconds per side or until crisp but not browned. Remove from oven. *Reduce oven temperature to 400°F.* Spread bean mixture evenly over each tortilla. Top with chicken mixture and cheese. Bake 5 minutes.

4. *Turn oven to broil.* Broil tortillas 2 to 3 minutes or until cheese melts. Do not let tortilla edges burn. Top with remaining cilantro. Serve immediately.

Makes 8 servings

ROAST BEEF WRAPPERS

½ **cup whipped cream cheese**

2 **tablespoons mayonnaise**

1 **to 2 teaspoons prepared horseradish**

Salt and black pepper

4 **(8-inch) flour tortillas**

4 **green leaf lettuce leaves**

½ **red onion, thinly sliced**

½ **pound deli sliced roast beef**

1 **tomato, thinly sliced**

1. Combine cream cheese, mayonnaise and horseradish in small bowl. Season with salt and pepper; mix well. Wrap tortillas in paper towels. Microwave on HIGH 20 seconds to soften slightly.

2. Divide cream cheese mixture evenly among tortillas. Spread, leaving 1-inch border. Divide lettuce, onion, roast beef and tomato among tortillas.

3. Roll up tortillas; wrap in plastic wrap. Refrigerate 30 minutes; cut in half to serve.

Makes 4 servings

CHICKEN PICANTE PIZZAS

6 flour tortillas (8-inch)
   Vegetable cooking spray
1 jar (16 ounces) PACE®
   Picante Sauce
1½ cups cubed cooked
   chicken
1½ cups shredded Monterey
   Jack cheese (about
   6 ounces)
3 green onions, sliced
   (about 6 tablespoons)

1. Heat the oven to 450°F. Place the tortillas onto **2** baking sheets. Spray the tortillas with the cooking spray. Bake for 5 minutes or until the tortillas are golden.

2. Spread **about ¼ cup** picante sauce onto **each** tortilla to within ½ inch of the edge. Top with the chicken, cheese and onions.

3. Bake for 5 minutes or until the cheese is melted.

Makes 6 servings

Prep Time: 15 minutes
Bake Time: 10 minutes

SUN-DRIED TOMATO WRAPS WITH FRIED CHICKEN

½ **cup ranch salad dressing**

4 **large sun-dried tomato flour tortillas, warmed, if desired**

3 **cups shredded lettuce**

4 **ounces sliced Monterey Jack cheese with hot peppers**

1 **can (2½ ounces) sliced black olives, drained**

4 **to 8 fried chicken tenders (about 1 pound), cut in half lengthwise**

Hot pepper sauce (optional)

1. Spoon 2 tablespoons dressing down the center of each tortilla.

2. Top with equal amounts lettuce, cheese, olives and chicken. Sprinkle lightly with hot pepper sauce, if desired.

3. Roll tightly, folding bottom; secure with toothpicks, if necessary.

Makes 4 servings

Variation: Add additional dressing on top of the lettuce, if desired.

TIP

If fried chicken tenders are not available in your supermarket deli, substitute frozen, cooked chicken fingers.

ROSEMARY PARMESAN CHICKEN FLATBREAD

1 package (11 ounces) refrigerated pizza dough

2 tablespoons sun-dried tomato vinaigrette salad dressing*

2 plum tomatoes, thinly sliced

1¼ cups shredded cooked chicken breast (4 ounces)

1½ to 2 cups baby spinach leaves, coarsely chopped

¼ cup grated Parmesan cheese

1 tablespoon minced fresh rosemary

If unavailable, may substitute with vinaigrette salad dressing.

1. Preheat oven to 400°F. Spray 15×10-inch jelly-roll pan with nonstick cooking spray. Unroll dough onto pan. Bake dough 5 minutes.

2. Remove dough from oven; brush with dressing. Layer with tomatoes and top with remaining ingredients.

3. Bake 8 to 10 minutes or until crust is golden brown. Cut into 12 slices.

Makes 6 servings

CHICKEN SAUSAGE, ARUGULA AND SWISS FLATBREAD

1 tablespoon light balsamic
    vinaigrette salad
    dressing

1 small onion, chopped

2 cloves garlic, minced

½ teaspoon red pepper
    flakes (optional)

1 (10½-ounce) stone-baked
    pizza crust*

1 fully-cooked chicken and
    apple smoked chicken
    sausage, diced

1 tablespoon chopped fresh
    rosemary

¾ cup shredded Swiss
    cheese

1 to 1½ cups arugula

*If unavailable, may substitute
with a 12-inch prepared pizza
crust.

1. Heat oven to 400°F. Heat dressing in large skillet over medium-high heat. Add onion, garlic and red pepper flakes, if desired, and cook 3 minutes; stirring occasionally.

2. Spread onion mixture evenly over pizza crust and top with sausage. Sprinkle with rosemary and cheese.

3. Bake 20 minutes or until crust is crisp. Remove from oven and top with arugula.

Makes 6 servings

TIMESAVING THAI WRAPS

1 package (3 ounces) chicken-flavored ramen noodles*

2 teaspoons creamy peanut butter

1½ cups packaged shredded coleslaw mix

½ cup diced cooked chicken

8 (6-inch) flour tortillas

Soy sauce (optional)

Discard seasoning packet.

1. Cook noodles according to package directions; do not drain. Add peanut butter, 1 teaspoon at a time, stirring until melted. Stir in coleslaw mix and chicken; cover and set aside 2 minutes.

2. Spoon noodle mixture onto tortillas. Sprinkle with soy sauce, if desired. Wrap and serve immediately.

Makes 8 wraps

TIP

These small wraps make a great light meal.

KIDS' WRAPS

4 teaspoons Dijon honey mustard

2 (8-inch) flour tortillas

2 slices process American cheese, cut in half

4 ounces thinly sliced oven-roasted turkey breast

½ cup shredded carrot (about 1 medium)

3 romaine lettuce leaves, washed and torn into bite-size pieces

1. Spread 2 teaspoons mustard evenly over each tortilla.

2. Equally divide cheese, turkey, carrot and lettuce on top of each tortilla.

3. Roll up tortillas; cut in half.

Makes 2 servings

PERFECT TURKEY & CHEESE FLATOUT® WRAP

1 Flatout® Light Flatbread

1 ounce fat-free ranch dressing

2 ounces BUTTERBALL® Deli Oven Roasted Turkey Breast, thinly sliced

1 slice reduced-fat Cheddar cheese

2 tomato slices

1 leaf romaine lettuce

Spread dressing over entire Flatout. On one rounded end, layer turkey, cheese, tomatoes and lettuce. Starting with layered end, roll up tightly. Cut before serving.

Makes 1 serving

Prep Time: 5 minutes
Total Time: 10 minutes

JAMAICAN JERK TURKEY WRAPS

1½ teaspoons Caribbean jerk seasoning

1 turkey breast tenderloin (about ¾ pound)

4 cups broccoli slaw mix

1 large tomato, seeded and chopped (about 1⅓ cups)

⅓ cup coleslaw dressing

2 jalapeño peppers,* finely chopped

2 tablespoons prepared mustard (optional)

8 (7-inch) flour tortillas, warmed

Jalapeño peppers can sting and irritate the skin, so wear rubber gloves when handling peppers and do not touch your eyes.

1. Prepare grill for direct cooking. Rub jerk seasoning over turkey.

2. Combine slaw, tomato, dressing, jalapeño peppers and mustard, if desired, in large bowl; toss gently to mix.

3. Grill turkey, covered, over medium heat 15 to 20 minutes or until internal temperature reaches 170°F when tested with a meat thermometer in the thickest part of the tenderloin, turning occasionally. Thinly slice turkey. Serve in tortillas with broccoli slaw.

Makes 4 servings

ASIAN WRAPS

8 ounces boneless skinless chicken breasts or thighs, cut into ½-inch pieces

1 teaspoon minced fresh ginger

1 teaspoon minced garlic

¼ teaspoon red pepper flakes

¼ cup teriyaki sauce

4 cups (about 8 ounces) packaged coleslaw mix

½ cup sliced green onions

4 (10-inch) flour tortillas

8 teaspoons plum fruit spread

1. Spray wok or large skillet with nonstick cooking spray; heat over medium-high heat. Stir-fry chicken 2 minutes. Add ginger, garlic and red pepper flakes; stir-fry 2 minutes. Add teriyaki sauce; mix well.* Add coleslaw mix and green onions; stir-fry 4 minutes or until chicken is cooked through and cabbage is crisp-tender.

2. Spread each tortilla with 2 teaspoons fruit spread; evenly spoon chicken mixture down center of tortillas. Roll up to form wraps.

*If sauce is too thick, add up to 2 tablespoons water to thin it.

Makes 4 servings

CHICKEN FAJITA WRAPS

1 **pound chicken tenders**

¼ **cup lime juice**

4 **cloves garlic, minced, divided**

1 **red bell pepper, sliced**

1 **green bell pepper, sliced**

1 **yellow bell pepper, sliced**

1 **large red onion, cut into ¼-inch-thick slices**

½ **teaspoon ground cumin**

¼ **teaspoon salt**

¼ **teaspoon ground red pepper**

8 **(8-inch) flour tortillas, warmed**

Salsa (optional)

1. Combine chicken, lime juice and 2 cloves garlic in medium bowl; toss to coat. Cover and marinate 30 minutes in refrigerator, stirring occasionally.

2. Spray large skillet with nonstick cooking spray; heat over medium heat until hot. Add chicken mixture; cook and stir 5 to 7 minutes or until chicken is browned and no longer pink in center. Remove chicken from skillet. Drain excess liquid from skillet, if necessary; discard.

3. Add bell peppers, onion and remaining 2 cloves garlic to skillet; cook and stir about 5 minutes or until vegetables are tender. Sprinkle with cumin, salt and ground red pepper. Return chicken to skillet; cook and stir 1 to 2 minutes.

4. Fill tortillas with chicken mixture. Serve with salsa and garnish, if desired.

Makes 4 servings

BUFFALO-STYLE WRAPS

⅔ cup **FRANK'S® REDHOT® Original Cayenne Pepper Sauce, divided**

4 **boneless skinless chicken breast halves**

¼ cup **blue cheese salad dressing**

1 cup **shredded lettuce**

1 cup **(4 ounces) shredded Monterey Jack cheese**

4 **(10-inch) flour tortillas, heated**

1. Combine ⅓ cup *Frank's RedHot* Sauce and 1 *tablespoon oil* in resealable plastic food storage bag. Add chicken. Seal bag; toss to coat evenly. Marinate in refrigerator 30 minutes or overnight.

2. Broil or grill chicken 10 to 15 minutes or until no longer pink in center. Slice chicken into long thin strips. In bowl, toss chicken with remaining ⅓ cup *Frank's RedHot* Sauce and dressing.

3. Arrange chicken, lettuce and cheese down center of tortillas, dividing evenly. Fold bottom third of each tortilla over filling; fold sides towards center. Tightly roll up to secure filling. Cut in half to serve.

Makes 4 servings

Prep Time: 10 minutes
Cook Time: 10 minutes

TURKEY PIZZAS

6 ounces lean ground turkey

1 package (11 ounces) refrigerated French bread dough

½ cup pasta sauce

1 to 2 teaspoons dried oregano *or* 1 tablespoon chopped fresh oregano

½ cup (2 ounces) shredded mozzarella cheese

17 slices turkey pepperoni, quartered

2 tablespoons grated Parmesan cheese

1. Preheat oven to 350°F. Spray baking sheet with nonstick cooking spray; set aside.

2. Heat medium skillet over medium-high heat. Add turkey, stirring to break up meat, until cooked through.

3. Unroll dough onto work surface. Cut into 6 squares. Place squares on prepared baking sheet. Spoon 1 tablespoon pasta sauce on each square; spread evenly to within ½ inch of edges. Top evenly with turkey, oregano, mozzarella cheese and pepperoni.

4. Bake 17 minutes or until edges are lightly browned. Sprinkle with Parmesan cheese.

Makes 6 servings

GO VEGGIE-STYLE

FARMERS MARKET VEGGIE WRAPWICHES

¼ cup **HELLMANN'S® or BEST FOODS® Light Mayonnaise***

4 **(6-inch) fajita-size flour tortillas or garden vegetable wraps**

4 **slices American, Swiss or Muenster cheese, halved**

1 **small tomato, cut into 8 wedges**

4 **cups cut-up vegetables, such as asparagus, red onion, cucumber, bell peppers, alfalfa sprouts or shredded carrots**

WISH-BONE® Balsamic Vinaigrette Dressing

Also terrific with HELLMANN'S® or BEST FOODS® Real Mayonnaise.

Spread HELLMANN'S® or BEST FOODS® Light Mayonnaise generously onto tortillas. Layer cheese down center of each tortilla. Top with tomato and vegetables, then drizzle with WISH-BONE® Balsamic Vinaigrette Dressing. Roll and fold filled tortilla.

Makes 4 servings

Prep Time: 10 minutes

STIR-FRY VEGETABLE PITA PIZZAS

1 teaspoon olive oil

1 red bell pepper, sliced

1½ cups (4 ounces) baby portobello mushrooms, thinly sliced

1 medium zucchini, thinly sliced

2 cloves garlic, minced

¼ teaspoon black pepper

2 (6-inch) whole wheat pita bread rounds

¼ cup pizza sauce

½ cup (2 ounces) shredded or grated Parmesan cheese

¼ cup chopped fresh basil

1. Preheat broiler. Heat oil in large nonstick skillet over medium-high heat. Add bell pepper; stir-fry 1 minute. Add mushrooms, zucchini and garlic; stir-fry 4 minutes or until vegetables are crisp-tender. Stir in black pepper; remove from heat.

2. Use small knife to cut around edges of pita rounds and split each into two rounds. Place on baking sheet. Broil 4 to 5 inches from heat source 1 minute or until lightly toasted. Turn pitas; top with pizza sauce, vegetables and cheese. Return to broiler; broil 3 minutes or until cheese is melted. Top with basil.

Makes 4 servings

NOTE: These pizzas can be cut into triangles and served as appetizers.

TIP

Choose zucchini that are heavy for their size, firm and well shaped. They should have a bright color and be free of cuts and any soft spots. Small zucchini are more tender because they were harvested when young. They should be rinsed well before using, but peeling is not necessary.

MEDITERRANEAN FLATBREAD

2 tablespoons olive oil, divided

½ cup thinly sliced yellow onion

½ cup thinly sliced red bell pepper

½ cup thinly sliced green bell pepper

1 package (11 ounces) refrigerated French bread dough

2 cloves garlic, minced

½ teaspoon dried rosemary

⅛ teaspoon red pepper flakes (optional)

⅓ cup coarsely chopped pitted kalamata olives

¼ cup grated Parmesan cheese

1. Preheat oven to 350°F.

2. Heat 1 tablespoon oil in large skillet over medium-high heat. Add onion and bell peppers; cook and stir 5 minutes or until onion begins to brown. Remove from heat.

3. Unroll dough on nonstick baking sheet. Combine garlic and remaining 1 tablespoon oil in small bowl; spread evenly over dough. Sprinkle with rosemary and red pepper flakes, if desired. Top with onion mixture; sprinkle with olives.

4. Bake 16 to 18 minutes or until golden brown. Sprinkle with cheese. Cool on wire rack. Cut flatbread in half lengthwise; cut crosswise into 1-inch-wide strips.

Makes 16 pieces

TORTILLA PIZZA WEDGES

1 cup frozen corn, thawed

1 cup thinly sliced
  mushrooms

4 (6-inch) corn tortillas

¼ cup pasta sauce

1 to 2 teaspoons chopped
  jalapeño pepper*

¼ teaspoon dried oregano

¼ teaspoon dried marjoram

½ cup (2 ounces) shredded
  mozzarella cheese

*Jalapeño peppers can sting and
irritate the skin, so wear rubber
gloves when handling peppers and
do not touch your eyes.*

1. Preheat oven to 450°F. Spray large skillet with nonstick cooking spray; heat over medium heat. Add corn and mushrooms; cook and stir 4 to 5 minutes or until tender.

2. Place tortillas on baking sheet. Bake 4 minutes or until edges begin to brown.

3. Combine pasta sauce, jalapeño pepper, oregano and marjoram in small bowl. Spread evenly over tortillas. Top evenly with corn and mushrooms. Sprinkle with cheese.

4. Bake 4 to 5 minutes or until cheese is melted and pizzas are heated through. Cut each pizza into four wedges.

Makes 4 servings

SAVORY FLATBREAD

2 tablespoons olive oil

1 package (8 ounces) sliced mushrooms

1 (8- to 9-ounce) package naan bread*

2 tablespoons prepared basil pesto

¾ cup shredded Italian cheese blend

2 tablespoons sliced red bell peppers

You may substitute two 8-inch prebaked pizza crusts for the naan bread.

1. Preheat oven to 425°F. Heat oil in large nonstick skillet over medium-high heat. Add mushrooms; cook and stir 7 minutes or until mushrooms are browned. Remove from heat; set aside.

2. Place naan on baking sheet. Spread pesto in thin layer over naan. Top evenly with cheese. Arrange mushrooms and bell peppers over cheese. Bake 8 minutes or until cheese melts.

Makes 2 servings

Festive Halloween Flatbread: Using Halloween cookie cutters, cut shapes and designs from naan bread. Place on baking sheet. Spread pesto in thin layer over naan bread. Top evenly with cheese. Arrange mushrooms and bell peppers to create goblin faces or other Halloween designs. Bake 8 minutes or until cheese is melted. You can also create different designs out of the flatbread by cutting shapes for faces out of the naan bread.

Naan Bread: Naan bread is a leavened oven-baked flatbread that is popular in South Asian cuisines, especially Indian. It is often made with added flavors and spices and can be found specialty sections of grocery stores. An 8- or 9-ounce package of naan bread typically includes 2 per package, each about 9×7 inches.

FESTIVE HALLOWEEN FLATBREAD

MEDITERRANEAN PITA PIZZAS

2 (8-inch) pita bread rounds

1 teaspoon olive oil

1 cup canned cannellini
beans, rinsed and
drained

2 teaspoons lemon juice

2 cloves garlic, minced

½ cup thinly sliced radicchio
or escarole lettuce
(optional)

½ cup chopped seeded
tomato

½ cup finely chopped red
onion

¼ cup (1 ounce) crumbled
feta cheese

2 tablespoons sliced pitted
black olives

1. Preheat oven to 450°F. Arrange pita rounds on baking sheet; brush tops with oil. Bake 6 minutes.

2. Meanwhile, place beans in small bowl; mash lightly with fork. Stir in lemon juice and garlic.

3. Spread bean mixture evenly on pita rounds to within ½ inch of edges. Top with radicchio, if desired, tomato, onion, feta and olives. Bake 5 minutes or until toppings are thoroughly heated and crust is crisp. Cut into wedges; serve hot.

Makes 8 servings

VEGGIE PIZZA PITAS

2 whole wheat pita bread rounds, cut in half horizontally (to make 4 rounds)

¼ cup pizza sauce

1 teaspoon dried basil

⅛ teaspoon red pepper flakes (optional)

1 cup sliced mushrooms

½ cup thinly sliced green bell pepper

½ cup thinly sliced red onion

1 cup (4 ounces) shredded mozzarella cheese

2 teaspoons grated Parmesan cheese

1. Preheat oven to 475°F.

2. Arrange pita rounds, rough sides up, in single layer on large nonstick baking sheet. Spread 1 tablespoon pizza sauce evenly over each round to within ¼ inch of edge. Sprinkle with basil and red pepper flakes, if desired. Top with mushrooms, bell pepper and onion. Sprinkle with mozzarella cheese.

3. Bake 5 minutes or until mozzarella cheese is melted. Sprinkle ½ teaspoon Parmesan cheese over each round.

Makes 4 servings

Note: These pitas can be served as appetizers, as well.

SOUTHWESTERN FLATBREAD WITH BLACK BEANS AND CORN

¼ cup prepared green chile enchilada sauce

2 oval flatbreads, each about 7½×11 inches

2 cups (8 ounces) shredded Monterey Jack cheese

1 can (about 14 ounces) black beans, rinsed and drained

1 cup frozen corn, thawed

½ cup finely diced red onion

½ teaspoon kosher salt

1 teaspoon olive oil

2 tablespoons fresh chopped cilantro

1 avocado, diced

Lime wedges (optional)

1. Preheat oven to 425°F. Place wire rack on top of baking sheet.

2. Spread enchilada sauce evenly on top of each flatbread, sprinkle evenly with cheese. Combine beans, corn, onion, salt and oil in medium bowl. Layer mixture on top of cheese. Place flatbreads on baking sheet. Bake 12 minutes or until flatbread is golden and crisp, and cheese is melted. Remove from oven. Sprinkle with cilantro and avocado.

3. Cut each flatbread crosswise into four pieces. Serve with lime wedges, if desired.

Makes 4 servings

PIZZA BAGELS

6 frozen, thawed or fresh
  bagels *or* English
  muffins, halved and
  toasted

1½ cups RAGÚ® OLD WORLD
  STYLE® Pasta Sauce *or*
  1 jar (14 ounces) RAGÚ®
  PIZZA QUICK® Sauce

¾ cup shredded mozzarella
  cheese (about 3 ounces)

Pizza Toppings* (optional)

*Use sliced pepperoni, turkey
pepperoni, mushrooms, bell
peppers, cherry tomatoes and/or
pitted ripe olives.*

1. Preheat oven to 350°F. Arrange bagel halves on ungreased baking sheet. Evenly spread RAGÚ® OLD WORLD STYLE® Pasta Sauce on each half, then top with cheese and Pizza Toppings.

2. Bake 10 minutes or until cheese is melted.

Makes 12 servings

Note: Recipe can be halved.

Prep Time: 5 minutes
Cook Time: 10 minutes

MUSHROOM & GOAT CHEESE PIZZA

1 package (about 14 ounces) refrigerated pizza dough

2 tablespoons olive oil

1 red onion, thinly sliced

3 cloves garlic, minced

1 package (8 ounces) sliced button mushrooms

1 package (6 ounces) sliced cremini mushrooms

1 package (5 ounces) sliced shiitake mushrooms

Salt and black pepper

1 package (4 ounces) goat cheese, softened

2 cups (8 ounces) shredded mozzarella cheese or pizza cheese blend, divided

¾ cup sun-dried tomatoes (not packed in oil), finely chopped

1. Preheat oven to 400°F. Spray baking sheet with nonstick cooking spray. Shape dough into large rectangle on prepared baking sheet. Bake 7 minutes or until set. Cool slightly.

2. Meanwhile, heat oil in 12-inch skillet over medium-high heat. Add onion; cook and stir 2 minutes. Add garlic; cook and stir 30 seconds. Add button and cremini mushrooms. Cook 5 minutes, stirring occasionally. Add shiitake mushrooms; season with salt and pepper. Cook 10 minutes or until liquid has evaporated.

3. Spread goat cheese on pizza crust. Sprinkle with 1½ cups mozzarella cheese and tomatoes. Top with mushroom mixture. Sprinkle with remaining ½ cup mozzarella cheese.

4. Bake 10 to 12 minutes or until cheese is melted and crust is golden brown. Serve immediately.

Makes 4 to 6 servings

TUSCAN VEGETABLE WRAPPERS

2 teaspoons olive oil

1 large onion, thinly sliced

2 red, yellow or green bell peppers, thinly sliced

1 package (10 ounces) sliced mushrooms

1½ cups RAGÚ® OLD WORLD STYLE® Pasta Sauce *or* RAGÚ® Light Pasta Sauce

⅛ teaspoon ground black pepper

1 package (12 ounces) flour tortillas, warmed

2 tablespoons grated Parmesan cheese

1. Heat olive oil in 12-inch nonstick skillet over medium-high heat and cook onion, red pepper and mushrooms, stirring occasionally, 10 minutes or until vegetables are tender. Stir in Pasta Sauce and black pepper. Bring to a boil over high heat. Reduce heat to low and simmer 5 minutes.

2. Evenly spoon about ⅓ cup vegetable mixture onto tortillas, sprinkle with cheese, then roll. To serve, arrange seam side down on serving plate and top with remaining vegetable mixture.

Makes 6 servings

Prep Time: 10 minutes
Cook Time: 20 minutes

TIP

Your family may not be up for an all veggie wrap so feel free to toss in some leftover chicken.

PEPPER PITA PIZZAS

1 teaspoon olive oil

1 medium onion, thinly sliced

1 medium red bell pepper, cut into thin strips

1 medium green bell pepper, cut into thin strips

4 cloves garlic, minced

2 tablespoons minced fresh basil *or* 2 teaspoons dried basil

1 tablespoon minced fresh oregano *or* 1 teaspoon dried oregano

2 Italian plum tomatoes, coarsely chopped

4 (6-inch) pita bread rounds

1 cup (4 ounces) shredded Monterey Jack cheese

1. Preheat oven to 425°F. Heat olive oil in medium nonstick skillet over medium heat until hot. Add onion, bell peppers, garlic, basil and oregano. Partially cover and cook 5 minutes or until tender, stirring occasionally. Add tomatoes. Partially cover and cook 3 minutes.

2. Place pita rounds on baking sheet. Divide tomato mixture evenly among pitas; top each with ¼ cup cheese. Bake 5 minutes or until cheese is melted.

Makes 4 servings

SWEET ENDINGS

FRUIT TART

CRUST

- 2 whole wheat naan (6 ounces total), torn into large pieces
- 3 tablespoons sugar
- 4 tablespoons melted butter

FILLING

- 8 ounces cream cheese, cut into 1-inch cubes, softened
- 3 tablespoons sugar
- 1 tablespoon lemon juice
- 1 teaspoon vanilla

TOPPING

- 2 kiwi, peeled and sliced
  Assorted fresh berries
- 2 tablespoons apricot jam, warmed

1. Preheat oven to 350°F. Line baking sheet with parchment paper; place 9-inch round fluted tart pan on top.

2. Place naan pieces in food processor fitted with metal blade. Process until fine crumbs form, yielding about 2 cups. Add sugar, pulse to incorporate. Add butter, pulse until combined, about 15 pulses.

3. Press crumbs firmly in bottom and up sides of tart pan. Bake 25 to 30 minutes until crust is set and golden brown. Place on wire rack; cool completely.

4. Beat cream cheese, sugar, lemon juice and vanilla on medium speed of electric mixer using paddle attachment 30 seconds. Pour filling into cooled tart shell, smoothing evenly with spatula.

5. Arrange kiwi and berries on top of tart. Brush fruit with warmed jam. Refrigerate 20 minutes before serving.

Makes 8 to 10 servings

CINNAMON-SUGAR TRIANGLES WITH CARAMELIZED BANANAS

2 pocketless pita-style round flatbreads

2 tablespoons melted unsalted butter

1 tablespoon granulated sugar

¼ teaspoon ground cinnamon

1 tablespoon packed brown sugar

⅛ teaspoon salt

1 large banana, cut into ⅛-inch-thick slices

Vanilla ice cream (optional)

1. Brush both sides of pita with butter (you will not use it all). Combine sugar and cinnamon in small bowl; sprinkle over one side of each pita.

2. Heat large nonstick skillet over medium-high heat. Working one at a time, place pita in skillet, cinnamon-sugar side up; cook 1 to 2 minutes or until bottom is golden brown and crisp. Turn and cook 1 minute until sugar is caramelized but not burned. Transfer to cutting board.

3. Reduce heat to medium, add remaining butter, brown sugar and salt. Cook 30 seconds until mixture is blended. Add banana; cook 1 minute until tender. Pour half of bananas over each pita; cut each into 6 wedges. Serve with ice cream, if desired.

Makes 4 servings

MIXED BERRY DESSERT LAVASH WITH HONEYED MASCARPONE

1½ cups assorted mixed fresh berries

2 tablespoons honey, divided

½ teaspoon vanilla

1 piece lavash bread, 7½ × 9½ inches

1 tablespoon melted butter

4 ounces (½ cup) mascarpone cheese

1 tablespoon julienned fresh mint leaves

1. Preheat oven to 350°F. Line baking sheet with parchment paper.

2. Place berries in medium bowl; stir in 1 tablespoon honey and vanilla. Refrigerate until ready to use.

3. Brush both sides lavash with butter; cut into 4 even pieces. Place on prepared baking sheet. Bake 10 minutes, turning half way through baking, until lavash is golden and crisp. Cool on baking sheet 5 minutes; transfer to wire rack to cool completely.

4. Stir mascarpone and remaining 1 tablespoon honey in small bowl. Spread over each piece lavash. Top with sweetened berries. Sprinkle with mint to serve.

Makes 4 servings

ROCKY ROAD SQUARES

2 pieces lavash bread, each
9½×11 inches

3 tablespoons melted butter

¼ cup packed brown sugar

4 ounces finely chopped
bittersweet chocolate

¾ cup chopped raw whole
almonds

1 cup mini marshmallows

Coarse salt, for sprinkling
(optional)

1. Preheat oven to 350°F. Line baking sheet with parchment paper.

2. Brush each side lavash with butter. Place side-by-side on prepared baking sheet. Top with brown sugar, chocolate, almonds and marshmallows.

3. Bake 12 minutes or until sugar and chocolate are melted, lavash is golden and crisp and marshmallows are toasted. Sprinkle lightly with salt, if desired.

4. Cool 5 minutes on baking sheet; transfer to wire rack. Cool completely. Cut into squares to serve.

Makes 8 to 10 servings

APPLE PIE POCKETS

2 pieces lavash bread, each cut into 4 rectangles

2 tablespoons melted butter

¾ cup apple pie filling

1 egg, lightly beaten with 1 teaspoon water

½ cup powdered sugar

⅛ teaspoon ground cinnamon

2½ teaspoons milk

1. Preheat oven to 400°F. Line baking sheet with parchment paper.

2. Brush one side of each piece lavash bread with butter. Place half of the pieces buttered-side down on work surface. Spoon 3 tablespoons pie filling in center of each bread, leaving ½-inch border uncovered. Using pastry brush, brush border with egg wash. Place another piece lavash on top, buttered-side up. Using tines of fork, press edges together to seal. Use small paring knife to cut 3 small slits in center of each pie pocket. Place on prepared baking sheet.

3. Bake 18 minutes or until crust is golden and crisp. Transfer to wire rack; cool 15 minutes.

4. Stir powdered sugar, cinnamon and milk in small bowl. Drizzle icing over pockets; let stand 15 minutes to allow icing to slightly set.

Makes 4 servings

CARAMEL APPLE FLATBREAD

FLATBREAD

2¼ cups all-purpose flour

½ cup QUAKER® Oats
(quick or old fashioned,
uncooked)

1 tablespoon granulated
sugar

1 package (¼ ounce)
quick-rising yeast
(about 2¼ teaspoons)

½ teaspoon ground
cinnamon

½ teaspoon salt

¾ cup water

1 tablespoon vegetable oil

1 egg white

1 cup chopped unpeeled
apple (about 1 large)

TOPPING

¾ cup QUAKER® Oats
(quick or old fashioned,
uncooked)

⅔ cup firmly packed brown
sugar

½ teaspoon ground
cinnamon

¾ cup reduced-fat sour
cream

¼ cup chopped pecans or
walnuts

1. Lightly spray large cookie sheet with nonstick cooking spray.

2. For bread, combine flour, oats, granulated sugar, yeast, cinnamon and salt in food processor bowl; pulse machine on and off several times until well mixed.

3. Heat water and oil in small saucepan until very warm (120°F to 130°F). With motor running, add liquids to flour mixture along with egg white. Process until dough begins to form a ball; continue processing 1 minute.

4. Turn dough out onto lightly floured surface. Knead apples into dough. Pat into 14×11-inch rectangle on cookie sheet. Cover with plastic wrap* and let rise in warm place 40 minutes or until almost doubled in size.

5. Heat oven to 400°F. For topping, combine oats, brown sugar, cinnamon and sour cream in small bowl; mix well. Spread mixture evenly over top of dough; sprinkle with pecans.

6. Bake 16 to 18 minutes or until edges are light golden brown. Cool in pan 3 minutes. Remove to wire rack and cool 10 minutes. Cut into squares. Serve warm.

*To prevent plastic wrap from sticking to dough, spray wrap with nonstick cooking spray.

Makes 16 servings

INDEX

ACKNOWLEDGMENTS

The publisher would like to thank the companies and organizations listed below for the use of their recipes and photographs in this publication.

The Beef Checkoff
Butterball® Turkey
Campbell Soup Company
Dole Food Company, Inc.
Nestlé USA

The Quaker® Oatmeal Kitchens
Pinnacle Foods
Reckitt Benckiser LLC
Sargento® Foods, Inc.
Unilever

VOLUME MEASUREMENTS (dry)

1/8 teaspoon = 0.5 mL
1/4 teaspoon = 1 mL
1/2 teaspoon = 2 mL
3/4 teaspoon = 4 mL
1 teaspoon = 5 mL
1 tablespoon = 15 mL
2 tablespoons = 30 mL
1/4 cup = 60 mL
1/3 cup = 75 mL
1/2 cup = 125 mL
2/3 cup = 150 mL
3/4 cup = 175 mL
1 cup = 250 mL
2 cups = 1 pint = 500 mL
3 cups = 750 mL
4 cups = 1 quart = 1 L

VOLUME MEASUREMENTS (fluid)

1 fluid ounce (2 tablespoons) = 30 mL
4 fluid ounces (1/2 cup) = 125 mL
8 fluid ounces (1 cup) = 250 mL
12 fluid ounces (1 1/2 cups) = 375 mL
16 fluid ounces (2 cups) = 500 mL

WEIGHTS (mass)

1/2 ounce = 15 g
1 ounce = 30 g
3 ounces = 90 g
4 ounces = 120 g
8 ounces = 225 g
10 ounces = 285 g
12 ounces = 360 g
16 ounces = 1 pound = 450 g

DIMENSIONS

1/16 inch = 2 mm
1/8 inch = 3 mm
1/4 inch = 6 mm
1/2 inch = 1.5 cm
3/4 inch = 2 cm
1 inch = 2.5 cm

OVEN TEMPERATURES

250°F = 120°C
275°F = 140°C
300°F = 150°C
325°F = 160°C
350°F = 180°C
375°F = 190°C
400°F = 200°C
425°F = 220°C
450°F = 230°C

BAKING PAN SIZES

Utensil	Size in Inches/Quarts	Metric Volume	Size in Centimeters
Baking or	8×8×2	2 L	20×20×5
Cake Pan	9×9×2	2.5 L	23×23×5
(square or	12×8×2	3 L	30×20×5
rectangular)	13×9×2	3.5 L	33×23×5
Loaf Pan	8×4×3	1.5 L	20×10×7
	9×5×3	2 L	23×13×7
Round Layer	8×1½	1.2 L	20×4
Cake Pan	9×1½	1.5 L	23×4
Pie Plate	8×1¼	750 mL	20×3
	9×1¼	1 L	23×3
Baking Dish	1 quart	1 L	—
or Casserole	1½ quart	1.5 L	—
	2 quart	2 L	—